SPORTING CHAMPIONSHIPS
THE NBA

Michael De Medeiros

WEIGL PUBLISHERS INC.

Published by Weigl Publishers Inc.
350 5th Avenue, Suite 3304, PMB 6G
New York, NY 10118-0069

Website: www.weigl.com

Library of Congress Cataloging-in-Publication Data

De Medeiros, Michael.
The NBA / Michael De Medeiros.
p. cm. -- (Sporting championships)
Includes index.
ISBN 978-1-59036-691-2 (hard cover : alk. paper) -- ISBN 978-1-59036-692-9 (soft cover : alk. paper)
1. National Basketball Association--History--Juvenile literature. 2. Basketball--Tournaments--United States--History--Juvenile literature. 3. Basketball--United States--Juvenile literature. I. Title.
GV885.515.N37D4 2008
796.323'640973--dc22
2007012103

Printed in the United States of America
1 2 3 4 5 6 7 8 9 0 11 10 09 08 07

Project Coordinator
James Duplacey

Design
Terry Paulhus

CONTENTS

What is the NBA ?

The National Basketball Association (NBA) is the world's top professional basketball league. There are 30 teams in the NBA. Twenty-nine teams are in the United States, and one team is in Canada. At the end of the regular season, the top 16 teams **qualify** to play in the NBA playoffs. The top two teams in the league then play in the NBA's championship series. It is called the NBA Finals. It is played between the winners of the Eastern **Conference** Finals and the Western Conference Finals.

The game of basketball was invented in 1891 by Dr. James Naismith. He was a teacher at the Springfield Young Men's Christian Association Training School in Springfield, Massachusetts.

Naismith was asked to create an indoor game that would keep students active in the winter. He created basketball.

The Miami Heat won their first NBA championship in 2006. They defeated the Dallas Mavericks in six games.

The game Naismith invented had only 13 basic rules. These rules have changed very little since the game was first played. The introduction of the **shot clock** and the three-point play have been the only major rule changes.

Dr. James Naismith (center) based basketball on a game called Duck on a Rock. Players tried to knock over an object with a stone.

CHANGES THROUGHOUT THE YEARS	
PAST	PRESENT
The original NBA was made up of 11 teams.	There are now 30 teams in the NBA.
The original hoop was a peach basket.	The basketball hoop is a mesh net.
The backboards were made of wire mesh.	The backboards are made of fiberglass.
Any player could take a **foul** shot.	Fouled players take their own shots.

The NBA Championship Trophy

The NBA championship trophy is known as the Larry O'Brien Trophy. It was created in 1977 and named to honor Larry O'Brien. He was a former NBA **commissioner**. The NBA championship trophy weighs nearly 16 pounds (7.3 kilograms). It is made of silver and bronze with a 24-karat gold overlay. The trophy stands nearly 2 feet (0.6 meters) tall and looks like a large basketball hanging just above the net. The ball on the trophy is the same size as the ball used in regular play. The winning NBA team keeps the trophy. A new one is made each year. Each trophy has the team's name and year of victory engraved, or printed, on it.

NBA History

The NBA was originally known as the BAA, or Basketball Association of America. It was formed in 1946. The BAA was one of two professional leagues playing in the United States and Canada. The other league was the National Basketball League (NBL).

The first BAA championship final was played after the end of the 1946–47 regular season. The Philadelphia Warriors were the first champions of the new league.

In 1949, the BAA and the NBL merged. The new league was called the NBA. The BAA champions from 1947 to 1949 are included among the NBA championship teams.

The St. Louis Hawks played in the NBA final series four times before the team moved to Atlanta.

The Los Angeles Clippers and the Minnesota Timberwolves are two of only eight NBA teams to have never played in the NBA finals.

The first NBA game was played in Toronto, Ontario, Canada, on November 1, 1946. The New York Knicks defeated the Toronto Huskies 68–66.

The first NBA final was between the Chicago Stags and the Philadelphia Warriors. The Warriors defeated the Stags in five games to win the first championship in NBA history.

The most successful team in NBA history has been the Boston Celtics. The team has won the NBA championship a record 16 times. They have appeared in the NBA finals 19 times. From 1956 to 1966, the team won 10 NBA titles.

The Los Angeles Lakers franchise has won 14 NBA titles. The team was originally based in Minneapolis, Minnesota. That Lakers team captured five NBA championships while they played in Minnesota. The team moved to Los Angeles in 1960. The Lakers have won nine NBA championships since moving to California.

The Detroit Pistons won their third NBA title in 2004. They defeated the Los Angeles Lakers in the final series.

NBA Mascots

Most NBA teams have mascots that entertain the fans. NBA mascots must be excellent athletes. Many use trampolines and ladders so they can jump high into the air and slam the ball through the basketball hoop. Others perform trick shots. They can shoot the ball from behind their backs. Some mascots shoot the ball from center court and try to put it through the basket. "Moondog" (right) is the mascot for the Cleveland Cavaliers. He is named in honor of Alan Freed, a famous Cleveland radio disc-jockey. Freed invented the term "rock and roll." His nickname was "Moondog." Cleveland is the site of the Rock and Roll Hall of Fame.

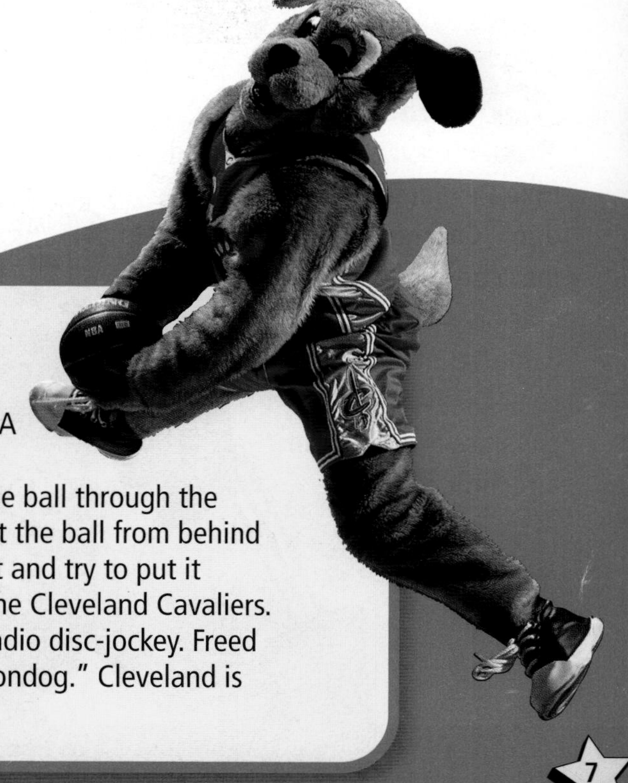

Rules of the Game

Basketball is a simple game. Each team tries to score as many points as possible by putting the ball in the other team's basket. At the end of the game, the team with the most points wins.

1 Time and the Clock

An NBA basketball game consists of four 12-minute quarters. The team with the ball must shoot the ball and hit the rim of the basket within 24 seconds. This is called the 24-second clock. It was introduced in 1954. After a team has been scored on, it has eight seconds to move the ball over center court.

2 Fouls

Players are allowed to five personal fouls. Players who commit a sixth foul must leave the game. If a player is fouled in the process of shooting the ball, that player is allowed two **free throws,** or foul shots. Each personal foul counts as a team foul. Each team is allowed four fouls in each quarter. After that, the other team is awarded two free throws.

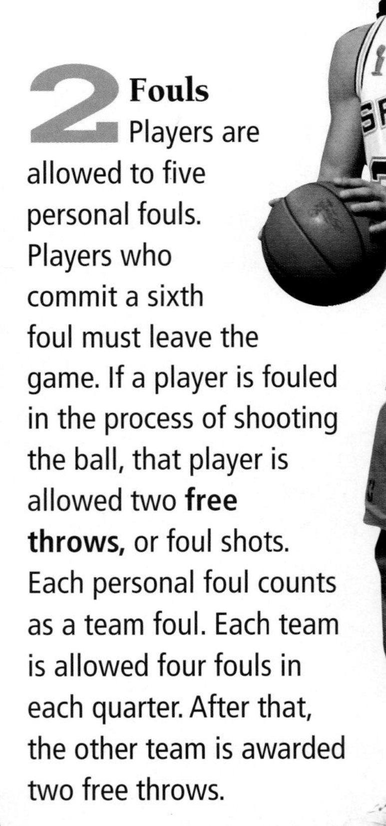

3 Conduct

Players are not allowed to hang from the rim of the basket after a **dunk**. Coaches are not allowed onto the court to argue rulings with the officials. Delaying the game, taunting, and complaining about penalties may result in a **technical foul**.

4 Dress Code

Players must follow the NBA dress code. They must wear dress shoes, a shirt with a collar, and dress pants when they are sitting on the bench but are not playing in the game.

5 Moving the Ball

Players must **dribble** when they run with the ball. Moving with the ball without dribbling is called traveling. The offending team must give up possession of the ball. Players cannot kick or punch the ball.

6 Players and Substitutions

A team must have five players on the court at all times. Each team has seven extra players, or substitutions. They can come into the game after any stoppage in play. A player who has fouled out of the game is not allowed to return.

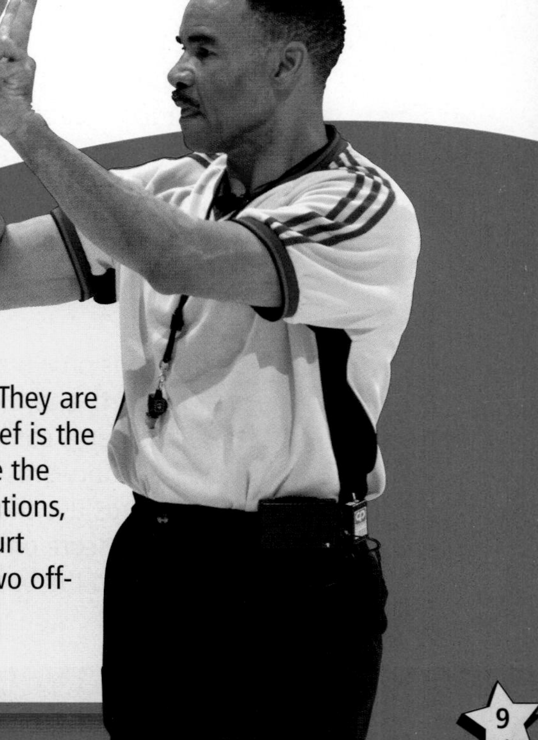

Making the Call

For each NBA basketball game, there are three on-court officials. They are called referees. One of the referees is the crew chief. The crew chief is the official in charge. All his rulings are final. All three referees ensure the rules are followed. They make penalty calls, keep track of substitutions, and make sure that all rules and regulations are followed. On-court officials inspect players' equipment before the game. There are two off-court officials. One official runs the game clock. The other official operates the 24-second clock.

The Basketball Court

NBA basketball games are played on a rectangular floor called a court. An official NBA court is 50 feet (15.2 m) wide and 94 feet (28.7 m) long. There are ten key areas on an NBA court. They are the backboard, the basket or hoop, the midcourt line, the backcourt, the frontcourt, the baseline, the center circle, the free throw line, the lane or the **key**, and the three-point line.

The backboard is 6 feet (1.8 m) wide and 3.5 feet (1 m) tall. The rim of the basket is attached to the backboard. It is 10 feet (3 m) from the ground. The hoop or basket is attached to the rim. The midcourt line divides the floor into two parts, the backcourt and the frontcourt. The backcourt is a team's defensive end of the court. The front court is a team's offensive end. The baseline is the line at each end of the court. It is the out of bounds marker. Players with the ball who step on the endline must give up control of the ball. There is a center circle in the middle of the court. This is where the game starts. The referee throws the ball straight into the air, and the centers of each team try to tip the ball to their teammates. This is called the opening tip-off.

The lane, or the paint, is the colored area in front of the basket. It is also known as the key. The foul line is at the top of the key. It is 15 feet (4.6 m) from the backboard. This is where foul shots are taken. A foul shot is worth one point. The three-point line, or the arc, is 22 feet (6.7 m) away from the basket. Any shot that goes in the basket from inside the three-point line is worth two points. Shots that go in the basket from outside the line are worth three points.

Players on the Team

There are five positions on a basketball team. They are point guard, shooting guard, small forward, power forward, and the center. Point guards set up the offense by moving the ball up the court. Shooting guards sometimes bring the ball up court. They take most of their shots from outside the key. Small forwards are accurate shooters. They often take more shots than other players. Power forwards use their size to move toward the basket. They are counted on to **rebound** the ball and score on close-range shots. Centers are often the tallest players on the team. They play close to the basket and usually **block** the most shots.

BASKETBALL COURT

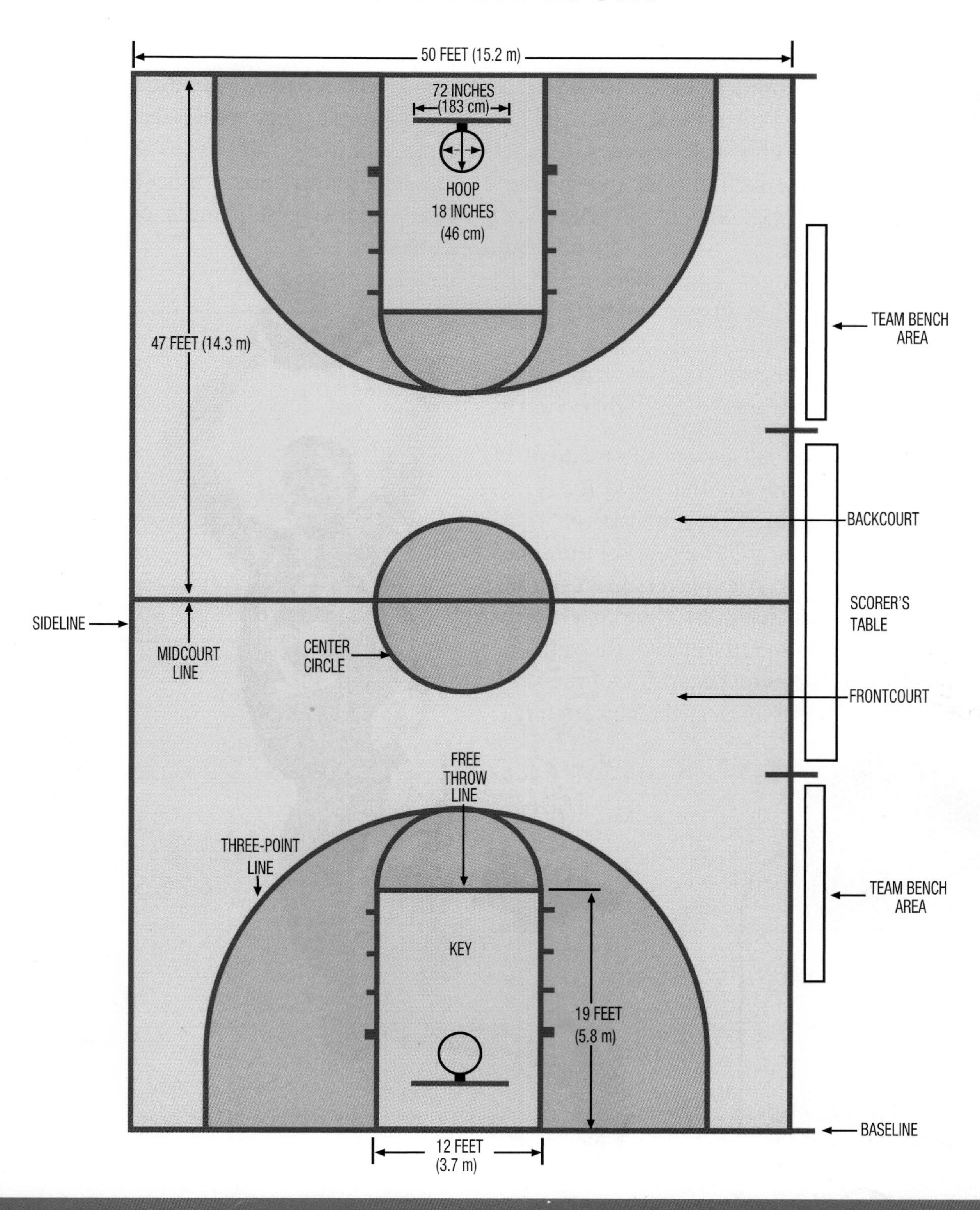

Basketball Equipment

Basketball equipment is very basic. All that is needed is a pair of running shoes and a basketball. Professional players use special equipment. They wear a team jersey, team shorts, and athletic shoes to play the game. There are rules as to the type of equipment a professional player can use on the court. The player's jersey must be tucked into the player's shorts. NBA Players cannot wear elbow guards, casts, braces, or any other hard object. Players may wear headbands, but they must be one color and no larger than 2 inches (5.1 centimeters) wide. Players are not allowed to wear jewelry on the court. They cannot wear anything that makes them taller or gives them an advantage over other players.

At one time, basketball shoes were made of canvas and had heavy, rubber soles. Today, shoes are lightweight. They are made of leather, nylon, or mesh. The soles of the shoes have special grips to stop players from slipping on the court. Many have ankle and heel supports. Basketball players spend much of the game jumping up and down. The inside of the shoe is cushioned to protect the player's feet.

GET CONNECTED

Learn more about the history of basketball equipment at **http://nbaballers.org/History.html**. Click on basketball equipment.

Players are allowed to wear headgear to protect an injury. It is common for a player who has a broken nose or a bruised jaw to wear a clear plastic face mask. Players must receive permission from the head referee before they are permitted to wear these types of equipment during a game.

Face mask

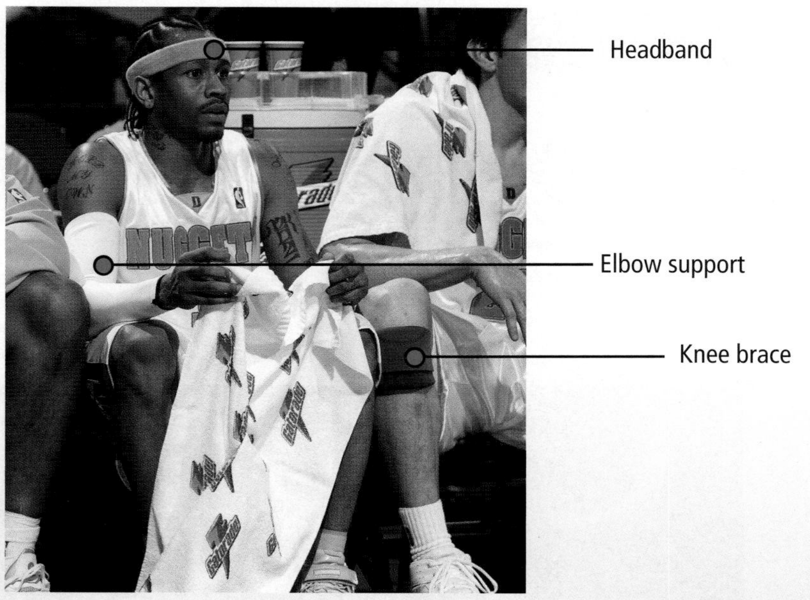

Team Uniforms

All NBA teams wear at least two different jerseys. Each team has a home jersey and an away jersey. Home jerseys are mostly white. An away jersey is usually colored.

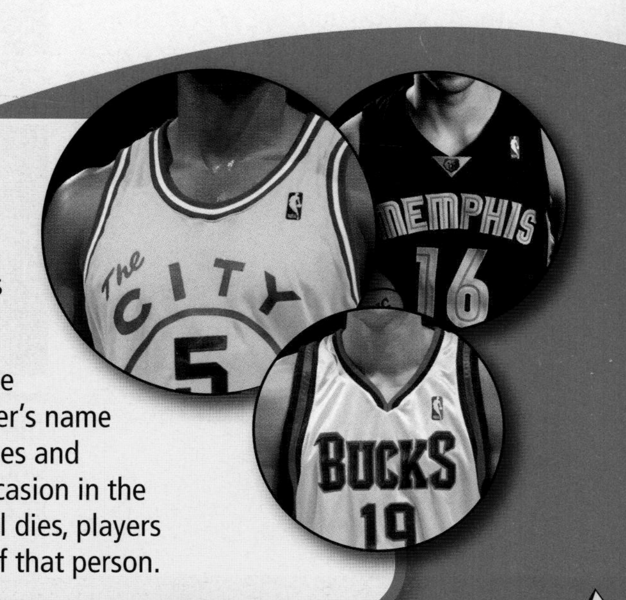

Player numbers are on the front and back of the jersey. The front of the jersey sometimes has the team logo. The player's name must be displayed on the back of the jersey. Special patches and symbols are sometimes worn. They represent a special occasion in the team or league history. If a former player or league official dies, players will often wear a black band on their jerseys in memory of that person.

Qualifying to Play

A team must win 12 playoff games before it can advance to the NBA championships. There are three rounds of playoff games before the final series is played. It can take two months to reach the championships.

There are two conferences in the NBA. Each conference has three divisions with five teams. The top eight teams in each conference, or 16 teams in total, make the playoffs. Until 2003, the opening round of the NBA playoffs was a best-of-five series. Now, each playoff round in the conference playoffs is a best-of-seven series. The first team to win four games advances, or moves on, to the next round.

The team with the best record in each conference gets home-court advantage in the playoffs. This means that four of the seven games are played in that team's home arena.

Having the best conference record in the regular season is important in the NBA playoffs. The top team always plays the team with the eighth-best record.

The Detroit Pistons defeated Milwaukee, New Jersey, Indiana, and the Los Angeles Lakers in the 2004 NBA playoffs.

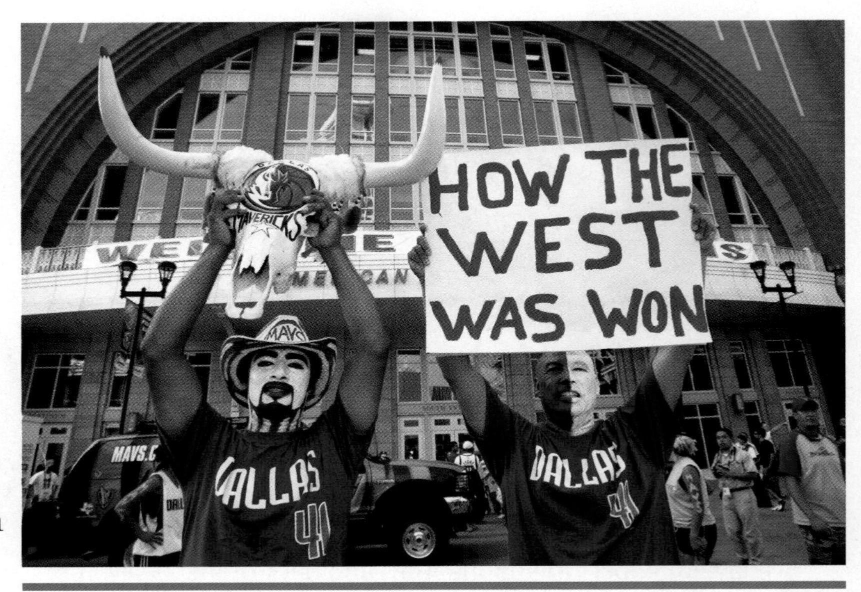

The Dallas Mavericks have qualified for the NBA playoffs 13 times since 1980. They won their first Western Conference championship in 2006.

The Boston Garden was the home arena of the Boston Celtics from 1946 until 1995.

Only three teams with the eighth-best record have been able to beat the top-ranked team since the NBA playoffs began in 1947.

The opening two games of each playoff round are played in the arena of the team with the best regular-season record. The next two games are played on the other team's home-court. The two teams then rotate from arena to arena until all seven games have been played or a winner has been decided.

The four teams that win in the opening round in each conference move on to the conference semi-finals. The winners of that series meet in the conference finals. The winning team of each series is named conference champion. The Western Conference champion and the Eastern Conference champion then meet in the NBA championship series.

Cinderella Team

Teams that do better in the playoffs than they did in the regular season are sometimes called Cinderella teams.

The 1980–81 Houston Rockets were a Cinderella team. They lost more games than they won during the regular season. The team was not expected to do well in the playoffs. However, in the first round, they beat the Los Angeles Lakers. The Rockets went on to beat the San Antonio Spurs and the Kansas City Kings. They became only the second NBA team with a losing record in the regular season to advance to the NBA championship series.

Where They Play

Dirk Nowitzki of the Dallas Mavericks helped bring the NBA championship series to the city of Dallas in 2006.

The location of the NBA championship series is not decided until the conference champions have been determined. The conference champion with the best regular-season record gets home-court advantage in the NBA finals.

The format of the finals is different from the one used during the conference playoffs. The first two games are played in the arena of the club with the best record. The next three games are played on the other team's home-court. The final two games, if they are necessary, return to the arena where the series started.

Wilt Chamberlain played in his first NBA finals with the Philadelphia 76ers in 1967.

Almost every team in the NBA has played in the NBA championship series. Of the 30 teams now in the league, only eight have not played in the championship round. The Los Angeles Lakers and the city of Los Angeles have hosted the NBA finals 22 times. The Lakers have played in the finals in three different home arenas. The Los Angeles Memorial Sports Arena hosted the finals four times. The championship series was played at The Forum, later known as The Great Western Forum, 14 times between 1967 and 1999. The Staples Center has hosted the final series four times since 2000.

In 2006, the Dallas Mavericks and the Miami Heat advanced to the championship round. It was the first time in 35 years that two teams who had never played in the final series met in the championship round. Miami won its first NBA title by defeating the Mavericks in six games.

Dwyane Wade of the Miami Heat averaged more than 34 points per game during the 2006 NBA championship series. This was the third-highest total in league history for a player appearing in his first NBA finals.

NBA CHAMPIONSHIP TEAMS AND NBA FINALS' MOST VALUABLE PLAYERS 1998–2007

SEASON	WINNING TEAM	LOSING TEAM	MOST VALUABLE PLAYER
1997–98	Chicago Bulls	Utah Jazz	Michael Jordan – Chicago
1998–99	San Antonio Spurs	New York Knicks	Tim Duncan – San Antonio
1999–2000	Los Angeles Lakers	Indiana Pacers	Shaquille O'Neal – Los Angeles
2000–01	Los Angeles Lakers	Philadelphia 76ers	Shaquille O'Neal – Los Angeles
2001–02	Los Angeles Lakers	New Jersey Nets	Shaquille O'Neal – Los Angeles
2002–03	San Antonio Spurs	New Jersey Nets	Tim Duncan – San Antonio
2003–04	Detroit Pistons	Los Angeles Lakers	Chauncey Billups – Detroit
2004–05	San Antonio Spurs	Detroit Pistons	Tim Duncan – San Antonio
2005–06	Miami Heat	Dallas Mavericks	Dwyane Wade – Miami
2006–07	San Antonio Spurs	Cleveland Cavaliers	Tony Parker – San Antonio

Mapping the NBA

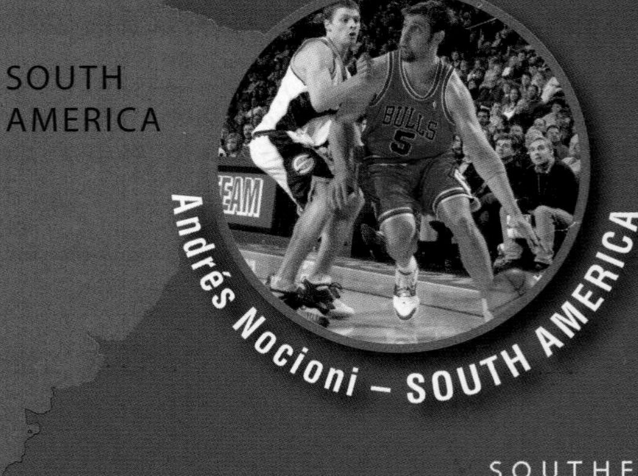

Every year, the NBA has a draft. Players from around the world are selected by NBA teams. This map shows where some of the NBA's top draft choices were born.

NBA FIRST ROUND DRAFT SELECTIONS BY CONTINENT 1997–2006
AFRICA – 4
ASIA – 13
AUSTRALIA – 2
EUROPE – 13
NORTH AMERICA – 235
SOUTH AMERICA – 4
N
W
E
S
Scale
621 Miles
0
1,000 Kilometers
EUROPE
ASIA
AFRICA
AUSTRALIA
PACIFIC OCEAN
INDIAN OCEAN
Dirk Nowitzki – EUROPE
Yao Ming – ASIA
Hakeem Olajuwon – AFRICA
Luc Longley – AUSTRALIA

Women and Basketball

Less than a year after basketball was invented, women began playing the game. A teacher named Senda Berenson read an article about basketball and thought it would be a perfect game for girls. She was the director of physical education at Smith College in Northampton, Massachusetts. Berenson wrote the first *Basketball Guide for Women*. These rules for the women's game were used until 1938. The court was divided into three sections, and there were nine players on a team. Each section had three players. The players were not allowed to move from section to section. This was known as "three-court basketball." In 1985, Berenson became the first woman to be inducted into the Basketball Hall of Fame.

Until 1971, women played two-court basketball with two guards, two forwards, and two centers.

The first woman's basketball game was played in 1892. The University of California at Berkeley played a game against The Miss Head School, a private school in Berkeley. Soon, women around the United States were playing the game.

Professional women's teams toured around the country playing games against men's teams. This was called barnstorming. One of the best-known women's teams was the All-American Red Heads. They formed in 1935 and played for more than 50 years. Another women's team that toured around the United States was Hazel Walker's Arkansas Travelers. They played together for more than 16 years.

Women began playing **full court** basketball in 1971. Five years later, in 1976, women's basketball was played at the Olympics for the first time. The United States won the silver medal.

GET CONNECTED

Learn about the history and growth of women's professional basketball at **www.wnba.com**.

The first professional league for women was the Women's Professional Basketball League (WBL). The league began play on December 9, 1978 and lasted three years. In 1993, the Women's Basketball Association (WBA) began play. Until 1995, this league played a 15-game schedule during the summer.

On April 24, 1996, the Women's National Basketball Association (WNBA) was formed. The WNBA has become the most best-known professional women's league. The WNBA uses a 30-second shot clock and plays with an orange and white ball. The Houston Comets have been the most successful team in the WNBA. They have won the WNBA Finals four times.

The Sacramento Monarchs joined the WNBA in 1999. The team won its first WNBA title in 2005 by defeating the Connecticut Sun in four games.

One of the Best

Ann Elizabeth Meyer attended Sonora High School in California. She was the first high school player to be named to the United States National Women's Basketball Team. She was a four-time All-Star at the University of California at Los Angeles (UCLA). In 1976, she helped the United States win the silver medal at the Olympic Games. Meyers was the WBL's most valuable player in 1979. She became the first woman to have a tryout with an NBA team, when she attended training camp with the Indiana Pacers. In 1993, Meyers was inducted into the Basketball Hall of Fame. She later worked as a basketball commentator on television.

Historical Highlights

There have been many unforgettable moments in the history of the NBA championships. Here are some of the moments that have made the NBA the world's best-known professional basketball league.

George Milken was one of the NBA's first star players. He could shoot both left-handed and right-handed. Milken won five championships with the Minneapolis Lakers during his career. In the 1949 NBA championship series against the Washington Capitols, Milken broke his wrist. He continued to play despite the injury. He averaged more than 30 points a game as the Lakers won the NBA title in six games.

In the 1970 NBA finals, the series between the New York Knicks and the Los Angeles Lakers went seven games. The Knicks' star player, Willis Reed, suffered a serious thigh injury. He was not expected to be able to play in the final game. Reed surprised everyone by starting the game. He scored two baskets on his first two shots before having to leave because of the injury. The Knicks went on to defeat the Lakers and win their first NBA title.

Elgin Baylor of the Los Angeles Lakers scored an NBA championship series-record 61 points against the Boston Celtics. He did this in game five of the 1962 final series.

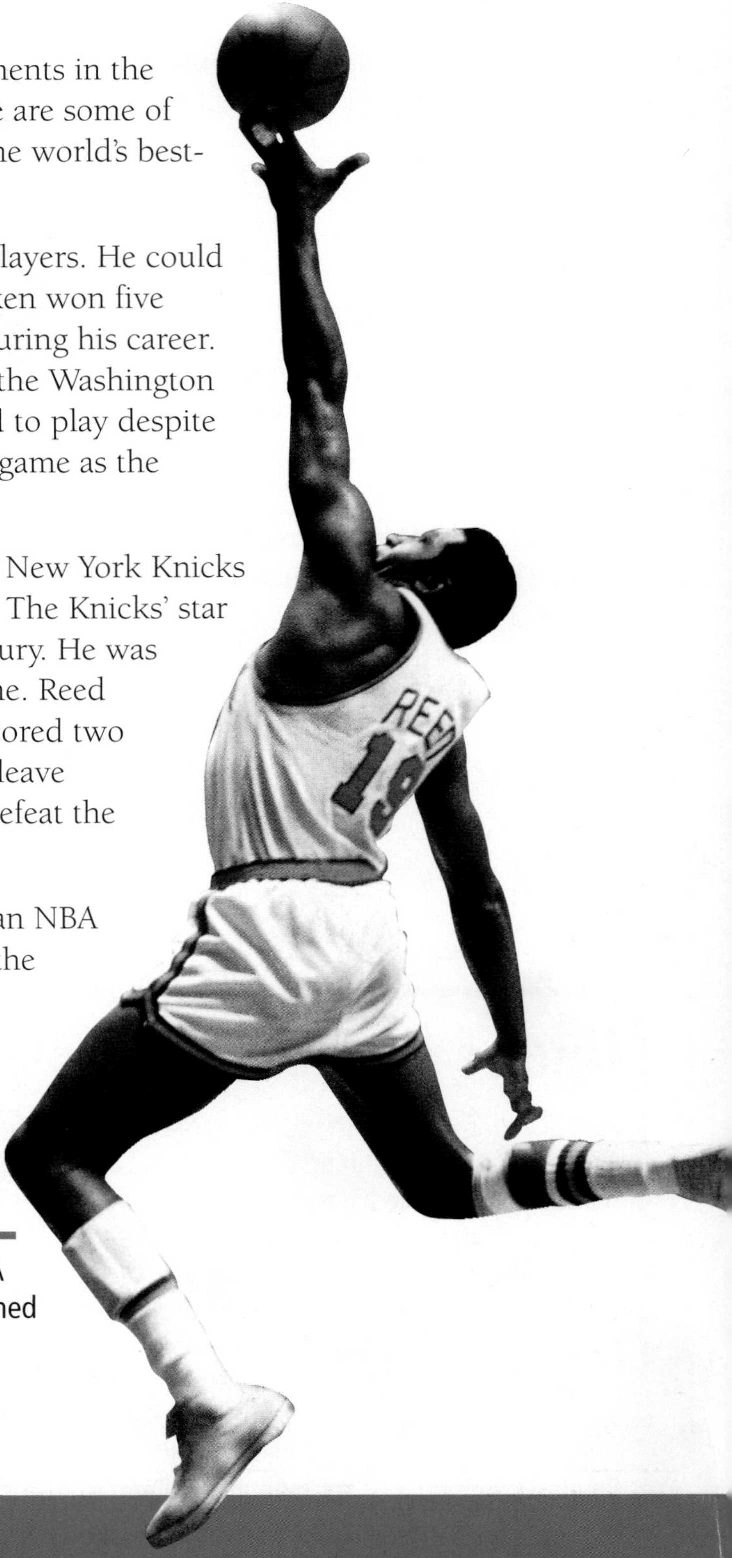

The New York Knicks won their second NBA championship in 1973. Willis Reed was named the NBA final series' most valuable player.

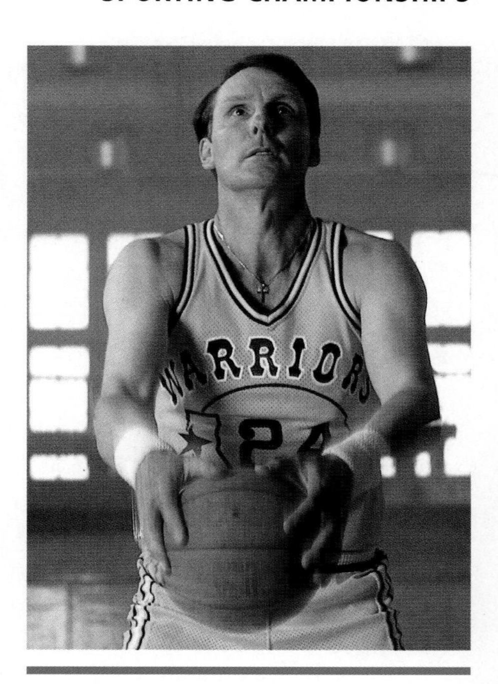

Rick Barry was one of the last NBA players to shoot foul shots underhanded, or from the waist up.

In 1980, the Los Angeles Lakers needed one more victory over the Philadelphia 76ers to win the NBA championship. Kareem Abdul-Jabbar, the Lakers' top player, sprained his ankle and could not play. A rookie named Irwin "Magic" Johnson was asked to play center. It was a position he had never played before in the NBA. Johnson scored 42 points, and the Lakers won the title with a 123–107 win over the 76ers.

In game six of the 1998 NBA final series, Michael Jordan made one of his best-known plays. With only seconds left on the clock and the Chicago Bulls trailing the Utah Jazz by a single point, Jordan stole the ball from a Jazz player. He dribbled the ball down court and hit the championship-winning basket. The shot gave the Bulls their sixth NBA title in eight years.

NBA CHAMPIONSHIP SERIES RECORDS

RECORD	PLAYER	TEAM, OPPONENT, AND YEAR
Most minutes played in a game – 62	Kevin Johnson	Phoenix Suns vs. Chicago Bulls, 1993 (3 Overtime Periods)
Most points in a game – 61	Elgin Baylor	Los Angeles Lakers vs. Boston Celtics, 1962
Most shots taken in a game – 48	Rick Barry	San Francisco Warriors vs. Boston Celtics, 1967
Most free throws made in a game – 19	Bob Petit	St. Louis Hawks vs. Boston Celtics, 1958
Most consecutive free throws made in a game – 15	Terry Porter	Portland Trailblazers vs. Detroit Pistons, 1990
Most three-point shots made in a game – 7	Kenny Smith Scottie Pippen	Houston Rockets vs. Orlando Magic, 1995 (Overtime) Chicago Bulls vs. Utah Jazz, 1997
Most rebounds in a game – 40	Bill Russell	Boston Celtics vs. St. Louis Hawks, 1960 Boston Celtics vs. Los Angeles Lakers, 1962 (Overtime)
Most **steals** in a game – 7	Robert Horry	Houston Rockets vs. Orlando Magic, 1995
Most **assists** in a game – 21	Magic Johnson	Los Angeles Lakers vs. Boston Celtics, 1984

LEGENDS and Current Stars

Kareem Abdul-Jabbar – Center

Kareem Abdul-Jabbar was born Ferdinand Lewis Alcindor, but changed his name in 1971. He was drafted by the Milwaukee Bucks in 1969 and won his first NBA championship with the team in 1971. In 1975, Abdul-Jabbar was traded to the Los Angeles Lakers. He helped his new team win five NBA titles. During his career, Abdul-Jabbar won six most valuable player awards and scored more points than any other player in NBA history.

Abdul-Jabbar was best known for a shot called the "sky hook." He would stand sideways under the basket, jump into the air, and hook the ball through the hoop. Since Abdul-Jabbar was more than 7 feet (2.1 m) tall, the shot was very difficult to stop. After he retired in 1989, he was named one of the 50 Greatest Players in NBA History.

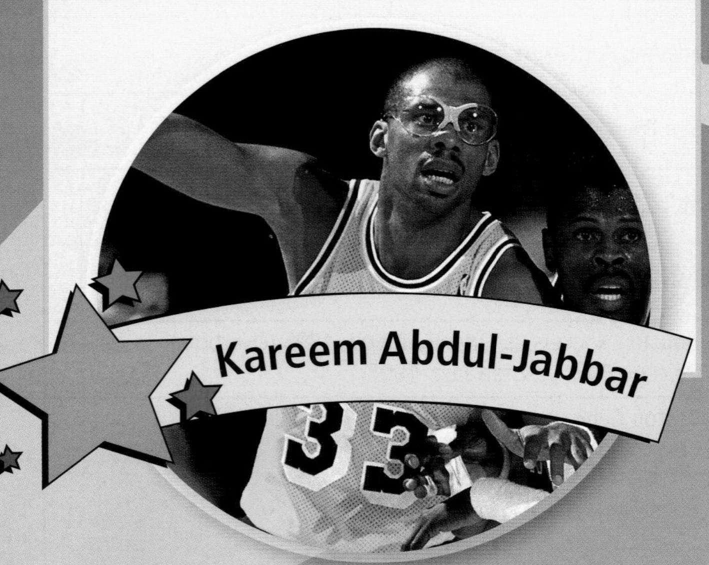

Kareem Abdul-Jabbar

Tim Duncan

Tim Duncan – Power Forward

Tim Duncan has won four NBA championships as a member of the San Antonio Spurs. He was named the NBA final series' most valuable player three times. Duncan did not start playing organized basketball until he was in the ninth grade. He quickly became one of the top high school players in the United States. Duncan went to Wake Forest University, where he was named the top college basketball player in the country.

Duncan is known as one of the NBA's best two-way players. He excels at both defense and offense. On offense, he has averaged more than 20 points per game during his career. On defense, Duncan is one of the NBA's top shot blockers. He has averaged more than 10 rebounds a game.

Duncan was the second player in NBA history to be named to both the NBA All-Star Team and the NBA's All-Defensive Team in each of his first six seasons.

Michael Jordan – Point Guard

Michael Jordan is often regarded as the best basketball player of all time. He won six NBA championships with the Chicago Bulls. Jordan was named as the NBA final series' most valuable player six times and was named to the NBA's First All-Star Team 14 times. He was known as a five-tool player. He had five different skills. Jordan could shoot, move the ball upcourt, pass, block shots, and rebound.

During Jordan's career, he was called "Air Jordan." This was because of his ability to leap higher than most other players. Jordan averaged 30.1 points per game during his career and scored 32,292 points in only 1,072 games. He helped the United States win the gold medal in basketball at the 1984 and 1992 Olympic Games. Jordan was named one of the 50 Greatest Players in NBA History after he retired in 2003.

Shaquille O'Neal – Center

Shaquille O'Neal is one of the biggest men to ever play in the NBA. He is 7 feet and 1 inch (2.2 m) tall and weighs more than 325 pounds (148 kg). His size makes him a difficult player to defend. O'Neal has played on four NBA championship teams and has been named the most valuable player in the NBA final series three times. Shaq, as he is called by most basketball fans, averages more than 26 points per game.

O'Neal is known for his play under the basket. He can easily dunk the ball and grab offensive rebounds. On defense, he can block shots and stop other players from getting to the basket. O'Neal began his career with the Orlando Magic in 1992. In his first season with the Magic, he was named the NBA's best rookie. In 1996, O'Neal joined the Los Angeles Lakers. He helped the Lakers win three NBA titles.

Famous Firsts

The first playing coach in the NBA was Buddy Jeanette. He coached the Baltimore Bullets and played guard for the team. In 1948, he helped lead the Bullets to the NBA title. Jeanette was the first player-coach in league history to win the NBA championship.

The first African American player in NBA history was Earl Lloyd. He played small forward for the Washington Capitols. Lloyd made his NBA debut on October 30, 1950. He joined the Syracuse Nationals in 1955. Syracuse won the NBA title that season. Lloyd and teammate Jim Tucker were the first African American players to win an NBA title.

Darryl Dawkins averaged more than five rebounds a game during the 1977 NBA playoffs.

Bill Russell was the first African American to coach in the NBA. As the player-coach of the Boston Celtics, Russell led his team to the NBA championship in 1969.

Darryl Dawkins was the first player to play basketball in both high school and the NBA in the same year. In 1975, he played for Maynard Evans High School in Orlando, Florida, and the Philadelphia 76ers of the NBA. Dawkins helped lead the 76ers to the NBA championship series in 1977.

The first NBA final series to be won by a foul shot in the seventh and deciding game was played in 1955. George King of the Syracuse Nationals made a free throw on the final play of the game. King's shot gave his team a 92–91 victory over the Fort Wayne Pistons.

Buddy Jeanette (right) was named the NBL's most valuable player three times.

The 1969 Boston Celtics were the first team to lose the first two games of the NBA finals and still win the championship. The Celtics won the NBA title by defeating the Los Angeles Lakers 108–106 in the seventh and deciding game.

On June 4, 1975, the Boston Celtics and the Phoenix Suns played the first triple-overtime game in NBA finals history. The Suns were down by 22 points at one time during the game. They came back to take the lead, but the Celtics eventually won the match 128–126. This game is considered by many experts to be the greatest game ever played in the NBA. Boston went on to win the NBA championship in six games.

John Havlicek helped lead the Boston Celtics to the 1975 NBA championship.

The first time the NBA championship was decided by a three-point basket was in 1993. John Paxton of the Chicago Bulls made the game-winning shot with 3.9 seconds left in the game. This shot gave the Bulls a 99–98 win over the Phoenix Suns.

The Dream Team

The Dream Team is the name given to the team that represented the United States at the 1992 Olympics. Eleven of the 12 players were NBA players. This was the first time professional players were allowed to play in the Olympics. The team featured NBA stars such as Larry Bird, Michael Jordan, Charles Barkley, and Magic Johnson. The only amateur on the team was Christian Laettner, a college player with Duke University. The team won all eight games they played, including a 117–85 victory over Croatia in the gold medal game.

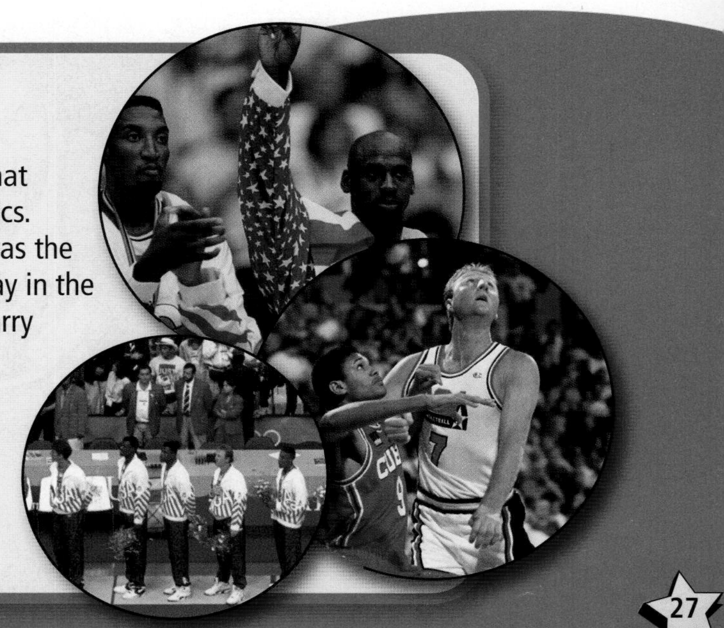

The Rise of the NBA

1946

Eleven teams are organized into the Basketball Association of America (BAA), creating a new professional basketball league.

1947

The Philadelphia Warriors win the first NBA championship. They defeat the Chicago Stags in five games. Joe Fulks is the leading scorer for the Warriors.

1948

The Fort Wayne Pistons, Minneapolis Lakers, Rochester Royals, and Indianapolis Jets from the National Basketball League (NBL) join the BAA.

1949

The BAA officially becomes the National Basketball Association (NBA).

1954

The Minneapolis Lakers win their third NBA title in a row. They defeat the Syracuse Nationals in seven games.

1960

The Minneapolis Lakers franchise moves to California and becomes the Los Angeles Lakers.

1969

The Boston Celtics, led by player-coach Bill Russell, wins its ninth NBA title of the decade. They defeat the Los Angeles Lakers in seven games.

1977

Julius "Doctor J." Erving joins the NBA's Philadelphia 76ers and helps lead them to the NBA finals.

1989

The Detroit Pistons win their first NBA title since moving to Detroit in 1957.

1995

The Vancouver Grizzlies and the Toronto Raptors join the NBA as the first Canadian franchises in the league since the 1946–47 season.

1998

The Chicago Bulls win their third championship in a row.

2002

The Los Angeles Lakers win their third NBA title in a row. Shaquille O'Neal wins the most valuable player award for the third time.

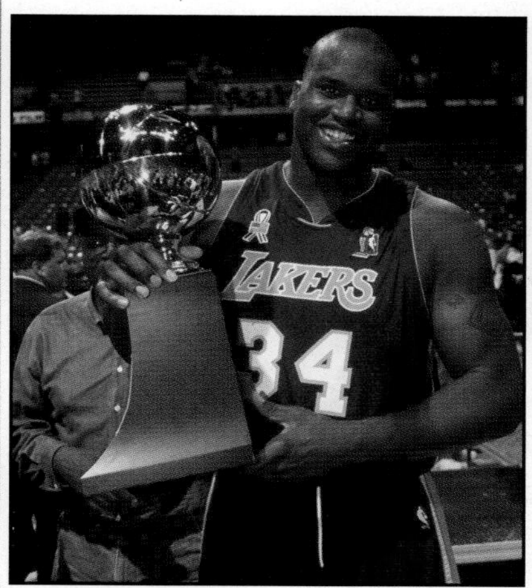

2007

The Los Angeles Lakers make their 54th playoff appearance, the most in NBA history.

QUICK FACTS

- The Boston Celtics won every NBA championship series between 1957 and 1969 except for two. They had a streak of eight NBA title wins in a row.
- The 1980s were dominated by the Los Angeles Lakers and Boston Celtics. The Lakers won five championships, and the Celtics won three titles.
- The Chicago Bulls, led by Michael Jordan, won six championships between 1991 and 1998.

Test Your Knowledge

1 Who invented the game of basketball ?

2 What were the names of the two leagues that became the NBA?

3 What team has won the most NBA titles?

4 In what year was the Larry O'Brien Trophy created?

5 Who was the first African American to coach in the NBA?

6 How many positions are there in basketball?

7 Where was the first NBA game played?

8 Who has scored the most points in NBA history?

9 When did women begin playing full court basketball?

10 In what year did the Dream Team win the Olympic gold medal?

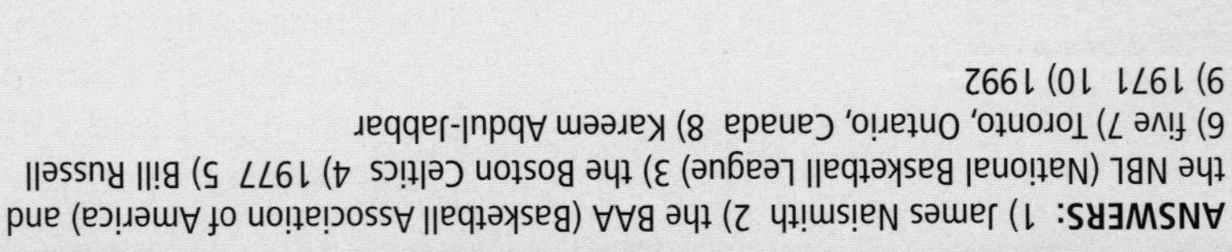

ANSWERS: 1) James Naismith 2) the BAA (Basketball Association of America) and the NBL (National Basketball League) 3) the Boston Celtics 4) 1977 5) Bill Russell 6) five 7) Toronto, Ontario, Canada 8) Kareem Abdul-Jabbar 9) 1971 10) 1992

Further Research

Many books and websites provide information on the NBA. To learn more about the league, borrow books from the library, or surf the Internet.

Books to Read

Most libraries have computers that connect to a database for researching information. If you input a key word, you will be provided with a list of books in the library that contain information on that topic. Non-fiction books are arranged numerically, using their call number. Fiction books are organized alphabetically by the author's last name.

Online Sites

For information about the NBA and the NBA championships, go to **www.nba.com**.

To learn about basketball in the United States, visit **www.usabasketball.com**.

To learn about basketball around the world, visit **www.fiba.com**.

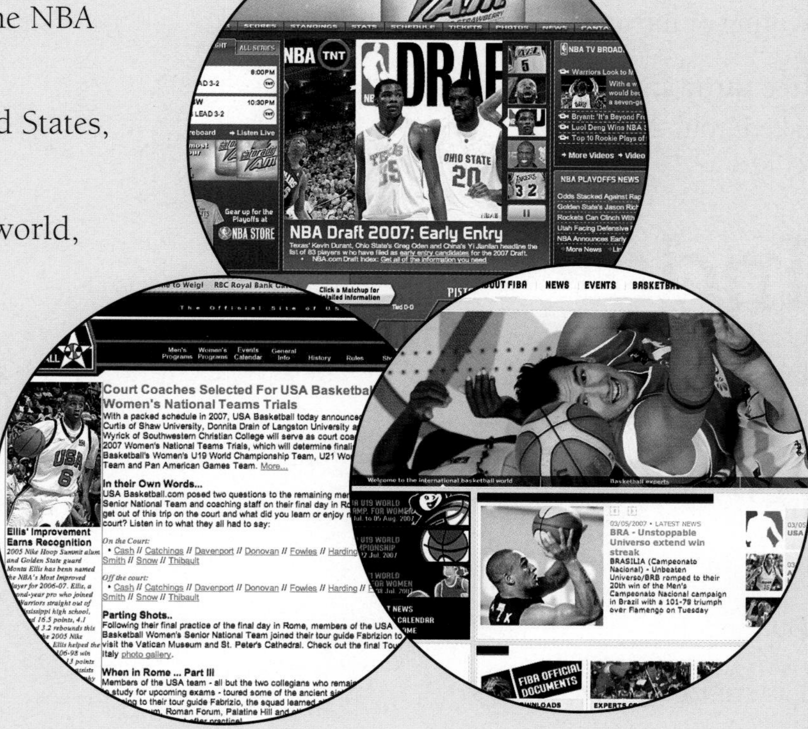

Glossary

assists: direct passes from one teammate to another that result in a successful basket being scored

block: to stop a shot before it has a chance to go through the basket

commissioner: a person appointed to regulate a particular sport

conference: an association of sports teams that play each other

dribble: to continuously bounce the basketball to move it up the court

dunk: to shoot the ball through the basket with the hands above the rim

foul: unfair actions that stop the opponent from scoring or moving the ball

free throws: open or undefended shots at the basket taken from the foul line, also called foul shots

full court: playing on the entire basketball court

key: keyhole-shaped area marked on the court near each basket, comprising the free-throw circle and the foul line

qualify: to be eligible for a round of competition by reaching a certain standard

rebound: to take possession of the ball after a missed shot

shot clock: a clock that indicates how much time a team has to shoot the ball at the basket

steals: to take possession of the ball from the other team

technical foul: violation of certain rules of the game, often involving unsportsmanlike actions

Index